Courageous Leadership

One hour to quash the tummy flies in your butter!

Diana Osagie

Courageous Leadership: One hour to quash the tummy flies in your butter!

Courageous Leadership Consultancy Ltd

Published by: Courageous Leadership Consultancy Ltd

England, United Kingdom

Visit the website

www.courageousleadership.co.uk

permission from the author, except for the inclusion of brief quotations in a review.

ISBN: 978-1-5272-4918-9

First edition, August 2019

Published in the United Kingdom.

Me?

Diana Osagie. Former secondary school head teacher. Present day coach, mentor, trainer and friend. Pleased to meet you.

I do the hard stuff; leading in challenging circumstances and advocating for those who don't have a voice. I'm 6ft tall and built like a barn door. I think I'm made that way on purpose, because you can sense the type of leader I am when I walk in the room.

I'm not brilliant at subtlety. I work hard, love hard and play hard. If I'm on your side, you WILL win. With me, it's 100% or nothing.

But, I'm an introvert and often prefer my own company. My ideal Sunday evening is spent with a pink G&T, watching Columbo on TV, and wearing my bunny rabbit onesie. On the flip side, my ideal Monday morning is back in the thick of leadership, pushing towards great things on behalf of others.

You?

At a guess, you're a leader, browsing through the sea of literature on leadership, and you've stumbled upon my book because of the lovely front cover (there's a certain captivating quality, don't you think?).

Perhaps you are totally courageous already and looking to add to your repertoire.

Or, possibly you are a little bit brave, but in need of a dollop of courage to get through this phase of your journey.

Maybe, you are utterly fearful and are wondering how on earth you were ever appointed to this role and worried about what you are going to do to succeed?

Whatever the case, this book is for you. It will take about an hour to read, so grab a drink and some Pringles, and dive right in.

Caveats.

I have changed some names.

I have changed some titles.

I have changed some dates.

That's it, the rest is all as it was – and as
it still is.

However, this is real life and I'm telling
my story, so if you recognise yourself
within these pages, CELEBRATE.
Good or bad, at least I remember you!

Love and hugs go out to...

My God

My mum and dad

My brother and sister

My husband (very supportive - when the football isn't on)

My teams

My students

My governors

My wicked suede jacket that always made me feel invincible

My church crew

My shoes once (they have magical powers and make me feel sooooo good)

May I just say?

No one is ever self-made. Those who say so are LIARS and UNGRATEFUL. Everyone has accessed support at some time - seen or unseen.

A grandmother who prayed.

A spouse who had dinner ready, in spite of their own awful day.

The kids who went without a goodnight kiss and didn't complain because you had another late night.

A teacher who persevered so that you could become better.

A government that, for all its faults, maintained a free education system for you to access.

Come on now, nobody gets to the top without using a ladder, the lift or stairs. You don't have wings!

Rant over.

Why 'Courageous Leadership' - The Book?
Because I can reach only a few of you with workshops, keynote speeches and webinars. This book will take about an hour to read and I will pour into you everything I have learnt so far on leading with courage.

This is not the 'theology of leadership'. You can google that.

I propose to give you:

-strategies I have used that work in leadership.

-strategies I have used that were terrible (obviously don't replicate these).

-my own tale of leadership in a challenging setting and how I was able to navigate through it without dying or killing someone.

You'll get my heart, my tears, and my triumphs - all for £10.

Warning.

I write with honesty and humour, and I really can't be bothered to make this academically intellectual. If you want the truth about leadership and strategies to overcome the hard times (and a romping good read to boot) then stick with me. Anything else, google it.

Diana x

This is not a story book, but…

Going to the school hall, checking in with my students about to sit their exam… Sumaya stood in line, clasping her pencil case, fear etched into her 15-year old features. I held her hand, as she whispered to me…

"Miss, I have tummy flies in my butter."

I knew what she meant. Now was not the time to correct her (beautiful) use of language.

"I know, me too. Let's go in together."

I am not an expert, I am not polished, perfected or finished.

I am, however, a successful head teacher who doesn't mind sharing the lessons of leadership gained through challenging circumstances. Success comes with messy bits, and mine came with the stuff I got completely wrong as well as the stuff that went brilliantly. I'll share the lot with you, so take what is useful and leave the rest.

However, here's a bit I think I got right,

In the summer of 2016, after 16 years of senior leadership, I was able to articulate what I call 'The 7 Statements of Courageous Leadership'.

Each chapter reflects one statement. They are not sequential, so please dip in and out as you like.

The 7 Statements of Courageous Leadership

❖ I will always feel fear, but I will limit the influence that fear has on my actions and thoughts.

❖ I know the absence of strength is weakness, but that having strength under control is humility. My strength is under control.

❖ I can work on my own, I can work through others, I can work with others.

❖ I am human first and a leader second. I remember the importance of family, love, compassion and grace.

❖ Leadership has weight. I have the emotional and physical strength to carry it.

❖ I am accurate and exacting, so if it's going to be done… then let's do it right.

❖ I am relentless and consistent in the things that matter. I have developed insight, into what matters.

When they go low we go high

-michelle obama -

Chapter One

I will always feel fear,

but I will limit the influence that fear has on my actions, speech & thoughts.

September 2010.

Appointed to the post of Head Teacher.

I couldn't wait for that first training day of the new term. The one where the staff are all gathered together after the summer break, looking and feeling great. A new leadership team, a new vision, a new day… and I was at the helm. There was no fear. Countless training days, assemblies and staff meetings all under my belt. This was nothing different.

Yes, I was the head teacher, but I was still Diana.

"Let's do this." I said.

All was well, leadership was great.

January 2011

Oh my life! Christmas was rubbish and I dreaded going back to school. I had inherited a crazy financial deficit from the previous SLT and I found myself at the point of having to announce redundancies to a school community that had

NEVER experienced that before.

It all kicked off.

The nasty targeted emails and

letters.

The anonymous emails and letters

sent by staff to the local MP and

DFES.[1]

The anonymous emails and letters

to the Chair of Governors.

---

[1] The member of parliament (MP) for our area just happened to be the leader of the opposition party in government at the time...wonderful!
DFES – Department for Education and Standards...triple wonderful!

The open letters to the whole Governing Body, which began their narrative with, *"We the undersigned…."* You know the type I mean.

The fake smiles.

The endless notifications of yet another staff union meeting and the list of demands that would land on my desk the next morning.

Look, I'm a physical presence, whether I want to be or not. I can deadlift over 100kg, and I'm no shrinking violet. When I'd walked into a room, I'd become used to commanding authority, whatever the situation. Yet during this hideous time of January 2011, I flinched if my office phone rang. I was filled with dread at the thought of email notifications. Every day was painful, my head hurt, and my emotions were shot. I was simply scared, and panic was my default.

I became terrified of making mistakes; so much so that I ironically ended up making even more. I later found out that the staff had taken a sweepstake on how many grammatical errors they could find in my emails. Nice. I was scared of influential staff who were galvanising their more vulnerable counterparts against me. I was scared of losing my job. I was scared that in the midst of this, all my students would fail their GCSEs. I was scared that I'd be discovered as an inadequate head teacher and that someone would turf me out.

Though we can sometimes overlook the good things, I remember that there were indeed some members of my staff who were for me through all of this, and I will always be grateful for their love and support. These were the colleagues who could see that the redundancy situation was not personal, and knew that I just happened to be the head teacher at this point of the school's journey. Some even saw the effect this was having on me personally, even though I didn't realise they were watching. They brought titbits of food to my office, came and made me laugh with a quip, and a couple would just come and hug me without saying a word. I had phenomenal governors on my side, too; wise owls who knew what to do, and when.

But, I still had fear.

I want to tell you that I morphed into some kind of brave and imposing lion, who roared and shook off the fear by charging victoriously across the plains. I can't lie, though. I simply put my head down and got through it.

Colleagues; fear will always be there. It's a valid emotion and has its place. It holds you from straying into arrogance, believing you are above confidence. What I've learned to do is to acknowledge its presence and then say to myself (out loud, sometimes):

- Fear, you are here, but you will not stop me from doing what is right, just and fair.
- Fear, I will put the young people and the wider school community first. It is easier to cave into your silly or immoral demands, but I refuse to go there.
- Fear, you will not stop me answering the phone or reading my emails (yes, it really did come to that).
- Fear, you will not stop me going to the staff meeting with a good attitude. I am well prepared.

If influence means '*the power to be a compelling force*', then there must come a time when you say to fear –"The compulsion you have over me to act, think or feel a certain way has to end."

Just think on that for a moment. Not only professionally, but in relation to your life as a whole. There simply must come a time when you say to your fears, "ENOUGH". I promised that I would share my warts with you in this book, so here goes.

- I feared not being liked (I hadn't long come through a very messy divorce, and relationships were a sore point in my life).

- I feared being seen as incompetent.

- I feared that my background as a council estate kid and a non–Russell Group university graduate would be seen as a negative.

- I feared that others who I was leading knew more than me, and that I was the inept one. I remember an influential colleague sniggering that I went to Wolverhampton University,

whilst he'd gone to Cambridge –
and didn't we all know about it.

I came to a place where I had to tell
these fears, which were screaming loudly
inside my head, demanding attention
and nourishment, "ENOUGH". I had
to tell myself to stop crying on the sofa
in the evenings. Looking back, I wish I
had shared my fears with someone at
the time. A coach from the outside
would have been invaluable to me. I
should have sought advice and support
for myself earlier. Please make sure you
do this if any of this resonates!

I tried to be an all-knowing, forever strong, super head teacher.

Nonsense.

With all this going on, my mask didn't slip once. Inside, I was trembling for days on end, but I never allowed it to show. I smiled, I walked the corridors, and I greeted everyone I met. I did this quite deliberately, because one of the anonymous letters to the governors had levelled the accusation that I never smiled! I quickly worked out who wrote that particular letter and smiled at her the most, which probably terrified her. I power dressed. I worked late and I started early. I wore the leadership mask skilfully. Nobody knew what it was like. I shared the story with a few people later on, but at the time, I suffered alone. This was in no way the right or best thing to do.

Colleagues; suffering in silence is never necessary and is a foolish move. Suffering in silence does not make you 'resilient'. It makes you ill.

My advice?

First - Make it compulsory to have support for your leadership journey. Not through one of those tokenistic ad-hoc meetings, where you are 'mentored' by an 'experienced' colleague for an hour once a term. I'm talking about meaningful, accessible, confidential support. You owe it to yourself as a primary responsibility to ensure this is in place. Don't leave it to the governors or to your line manager to organise for you. Secure the level of support you will need to be successful in your leadership journey, and know that a good governing body or line manager will pay for it! If they don't, go right ahead and invest in yourself anyway! It will be worth it, much as the cost stings.

Second – If it scares you, whatever it is, admit it, share it, and deal with it. I had issues of rejection stemming from the divorce that caused initial fear in me, but it would be a cold day in Hell before I was about to admit that to anyone! It took me over a decade to deal with that inner fear – and by that time, I was remarried for goodness sake! I carried that fear inside me for ten years. TEN years! Imagine what I could have achieved if I had dealt with it in under one? I was naïve in thinking that I could push the fear of rejection deep enough into my soul to the point where it would have no effect on my leadership. I was an idiot.

Let me say this with all love and concern for you. Fear is like a cancer. It spreads. It is never contained to one area of your life, but will wrap its tentacles around you in all sorts of places, bringing about all manner of consequences as it tightens.

Why do I use the analogy of cancer? My dad passed away in 2007 from pancreatic cancer. He was diagnosed in the February, and was dead by April. The cancer spread in a way that took everyone by surprise. There had been signs, though. For over a year, dad had been complaining of not feeling very well. Nothing specific, just not feeling himself. When we asked him about it each day, it was clear he was merely learning to live around this feeling.

Unsurprisingly, malignant cancers very rarely (if ever) heal themselves. You have to intervene in a dramatic and convincing way to stand any chance of winning. You have to entirely negate the influence the cancer has upon the body. Sometimes, the treatment feels worse than the disease itself, but if you are not aggressive with cancer, it will do its utmost to regain its influential position and limit your life in its process.

"Whoa!" I hear you cry! *"Diana, that's a bit strong, likening internal fear to cancer, eh?"*

Yes, the imagery is strong, but I bet everyone reading this understands the potential power of fear now you have such vivid pictures in your head. You can see why it's vital that you limit the influence fear has on your life if you're going to make it out of this alive.

It's not about rushing around your organisation, baring your leadership teeth and growling via email. You need to deal with your internal fears so that you can lead without limitation. Fear of rejection stemming from my private life showed up in my leadership journey, simply by me not wanting to have those 'difficult conversations' with people. As a head teacher, this was a slight issue, as there is only so much you can delegate to your deputies. Oh, and also, I really wanted to be liked. The financial deficit was not my fault, and I didn't want my staff to see me in a negative way because

41

of the strong action I was forced to take. I wanted a pleasant working environment for us all to thrive in, but I didn't get that, and the toxicity was killing us all.

Over again in my head, the same conversation played out.

"But what if the unions rise up and call another strike?"

"But what if this gets in the newspapers and parents see the negative press?"

"But what if key staff leave purely through preference and choice?"

These fearful 'what ifs' plagued my mind for days on end. I danced around conversations I should have had because I was so deeply afraid. I didn't want to experience leadership rejection. I wanted to have the right answer, to every problem, every time, and to keep everyone happy in the process. My internal fear limited the early stages of my leadership prowess.

So now, do you get it?

Fear - don't play patter-cake with it.

Fear - don't learn to live with it.

Fear - don't ignore it and hope it goes away by itself. It won't. It will probably pop up at the most awkward moment, like when you hear a piece of music in the Year 10 assembly, which sets you off in floods of tears and you have to make your babbled apologies through sobs and exit via the fire doors.

Get support, deal with your fear, and conquer it.

Oh, by the way, I need to add a little bit extra to this chapter, because if I don't, I will never hear the end of it.

There was one member of staff in particular who stood with me even when the fire was at its hottest. He would turn up at my office and do anything to make me smile. He would listen to the little information that I was willing to share and was a true confidant. He refused to sign the 'We the undersigned…' letters, along with some of his peers. He came in to work on strike days and helped the Senior Leadership Team teach the whole of Year 11 to get them

through their exams. He saw the
woman behind the head teacher.
Always respectful, genuinely
concerned, he had my back.

So I married him.

Then I told him to leave.

My job was hard enough without having
to hold my husband to account in the
workplace!

I know who I am.

I know my strength, my worth & position.

I am a queen, I ROAR only when necessary.

My strength is under control.

Diana Osagie

Chapter Two

I know the absence of strength is weakness, but having strength under control is humility.

My strength is under control.

Let me tell you several stories that illustrate the second courageous statement I put forward to you in this book.

Story one.

As a Senior Leadership Team, we were grappling with the lack of consistency in our systems of accountability, as well as with the quality assurance of practice across the school. Some staff were great; setting high targets and pushing for the best on behalf of our young people. Others were there simply to collect their salary and wait for their pension. That may be harsh, but that's how it seemed to me.

A school consultant came into our lives and brought with her a system of accountability that revolutionised our work as middle and senior leaders. I had never seen anything like it and it turned our school into an efficient but graceful organism. Every leader knew where they stood, transparency reigned, and standards began to rise across the school.

Some of our middle leaders HATED it!

Under the new system, there was nowhere to hide, and with the level of support built into the system, excuses held no value. I grew to trust and rely on the consultant, as the impact of their work began to deliver my vision of high challenge with high support across the teaching and leadership practice of the school.

It got back to me that a new member of my senior leadership team had led a charge in discrediting the consultant, therefore aiming to have the accountability system also discredited and ultimately abandoned.

"But she has no internet presence! How can a consultant who is any good in business not have a website?"

"But she didn't go to a top university! How can a person lead academia if they're not an academic?"

"There are no recommendations or references to her past work, so where did she spring from?"

Just take a quick look back to the start of this chapter, with the picture of the lioness. She is sitting there serenely; full of courage. She is basking in the moonlight, just chilling. The potential for her to open her mouth, throw back her head and bare her teeth is always there. The claws are sheathed right now, but should she choose to, they will swipe and take out your throat.

Can I be honest?

When I heard what my member of so-called senior staff had been doing, I was ready to unsheathe my leadership claws and silence the threat with one perfectly poised swipe. I was about to roar – loudly - and nothing was going to prevent my prey from feeling the full force of my strength. I was about to click send on the email telling them to see me for a meeting, when I got distracted. Then I got distracted again. The whole day went by, and I was constantly busy, it seemed. Somehow, the senior leader got word that I was about to roar. I suspect it was one of my deputies who told on me – they knew me so well.

Here's what followed.

The member of staff in question turned up at my door of their own volition.

I looked up, and got ready to roar.

"Miss Osagie, before you say anything, I want to apologise wholeheartedly and completely for what I've said about the consultant. I was utterly wrong and it's a poor reflection of the senior team. It won't happen again."

I stared, open mouthed.

My roar had been quashed.

Damn, I was quite looking forward to that as well.

I took a breath and ask them to sit down. I could see the fear on their face. I didn't want my staff to fear me, but they needed to understand what makes me roar.

"You went against my values, and that is not something I overlook. The values of the school are everywhere, and they are the values we live by. Confidence, aspiration, respect and reflect. Your actions flew in the face of the respect we should all have for each other and I cannot have that. Everyone is valuable to me. I need my senior team to hold that same attitude, so if you want to serve alongside me, I need you to reflect on this".

They left, hopefully feeling better than when they arrived.

I'll never know.

Just because you can roar, doesn't mean you have to.

Just because you are strong, doesn't mean you must always display your strength.

Let your strength be under control.

Story two.

This one is hard to relate to you without sounding really dramatic, but I found myself as the head teacher somewhat held hostage by the skillset of a leader in the school! Even when I think back on this now, I still feel like a plum, but it's true, I was held to ransom and it was of my own doing. I put myself in that position without realising it.

Back then, our school data systems were very basic. Few understood how the programme worked and even fewer understood how to use data as a tool to underpin progress for students. Then, along comes someone who can 'do data'. It was like a golden unicorn had trotted in. From that moment, this person could do no wrong in my eyes. I was so desperate for their skillset to put things right in my school that I put up with shenanigans and foolishness from them that nobody else would dare suffer. It didn't go un-noticed.

I found myself very quickly in the situation of justifying rubbish from this leader to others, because I was afraid they might leave and I was desperate for them to stay. Behaving this way showed weakness in me and discredited my own leadership. Eventually, I woke up.

My golden unicorn announced that they were leaving unless they got x, y and z from me.

I listened, helped them plan, and then celebrated their exit.

The absence of strength is weakness. I should have been strong enough to secure support in the use of data from a neighbouring school or similar. I should have admitted that we were struggling and subsequently asked for help. I should have had the courage to ask internal leaders, *"Who is prepared to be trained in this field and then come back and train the rest of us?"* I should have been strong enough in the first instance not to listen to the one or two staff who *did* seem to understand our data, but constantly declared that what I wanted would not be possible.

Yes, we had the skillset of an amazing person for a period of time, but my weakness in not challenging the river of foolishness that ran through the school because of them is something I regret.

Story three.

This story still saddens me. It's an example of me flexing my leadership muscle and unleashing my roar when they were just not justified.

We had a teacher who was new to the school and new to the profession. This person was not a great teacher! It didn't matter how much support we put in place, they were still woeful. I couldn't figure it out. There was no obvious reason why this person should not be able to handle the classroom and teach their subject, but every lesson was a mess. They had to be forced to mark the students' books, they had to be forced to plan decent lessons, and the whole thing was ridiculous.

The details of a conversation this teacher had in the staffroom with another equally useless member of staff later got back to me.

"I can't stand these kids. I'm only here for the money, so as long as I get paid, who gives a xxxx what happens in the classroom. Once they sign off my qualification, I'm gone."

"Listen, they are so desperate here, they'll take anyone. Who wants to teach kids like these? Get paid, go home, that's my motto."

When this got back to me, I felt sick.

Then I felt angry.

Then I was enraged and so upset to the point that I went home. If I had stayed and happened upon the teacher (well both of them, actually) in the corridor, I probably would have lost my career as well as my mind!

The insult to me was one thing, but trampling on the values of our school was another entirely. And then, to denigrate my young people like that? Without us to advocate for them, those young people may never have had a chance of making it. They didn't have tutors at home, and many did not have access to adults who would support or promote academia in their lives at all. We were 'it'; the first and last hope. We had to be courageous on their behalf, pushing and asking for what seemed like an impossible dream, so that they could have a chance to live them.

And you openly declare you are 'only here for the money'?

I introduced this scenario by telling you that this whole thing saddened me. Why? It's not what you might think. When I reflected on it all, I didn't give that teacher a chance to sit with me and have a conversation about values. They did not pass the qualification, and this result was totally justified and correct, so there was no way I could say that they were ready to serve in our profession, but I regret not taking the time to control my strength and take an opportunity to have the deeper conversation. I was so angry that I just roared, swiped my claws and left. I treated that person with the same level of contempt they held for the school. That was wrong.

I had to learn how to handle my influence and carry the weight of my words carefully. This meant dispelling old narratives in my head that leaders should appear strong, bark at people, and never smile before the end of their first year. This caricature of leadership tried to rise up in my own journey, so watch out for it in yours.

Can I give you one more story? It's hard to resist this one…

One of my mentees narrated this to me and it's a classic example of a leader roaring when it was totally unnecessary, and ended up with them looking like a total numpty.

The mentee in question went for an interview and things were going well. The head teacher read through their CV aloud and noted that they had completed the Courageous Leadership course that I run for those seeking promotion.

"Oh, I see, you have completed this Courageous Leadership course."

"Yes, it gave me good insight into how leadership works and helped me to prepare for the next phase of my leadership journey."

The next question from any normal head teacher would have been something like, *"Tell me more about what you learnt and how this has helped you develop"*. But no... this head teacher wanted to flex some muscle.

"Well I hope you have no intentions of being 'courageous' at this school! Nobody challenges me, I don't allow it!"

Yep ... true story.

Don't confuse confidence and foolishness, attempting leadership on your own is foolish.

Get support.

. Diana Osagie

Chapter Three

I can work on my own.

I can work through others.

I can work with others.

Despite my headship responsibilities, I taught my own GCSE classes every week, every year. I was always given Set 4 or 5, and instructed by my 'boss' - the Head of Department - that all pupils had to pass. In my day, I was quite good at teaching, but I quickly realised that being the head teacher and retaining my status as a great teacher as well, was not a guaranteed partnership. I had some phenomenal staff, from young whippersnappers who could wipe the floor with me, to senior leaders who understood the heart of teaching. I was in awe of all of them.

It's relatively easy to say, *"You're a better teacher than me."*

It is another matter to say, *"You're a better teacher than me. I trust you to develop teaching across the school. I want you to develop teams, workshops and move our teaching practice to another level. I promise I will stay out of your way."*

I had the vision for success not just to arrive at our school, but to remain. So, teaching had to be good or better every day in every classroom. Some staff looked at me like I was crazy.

In the early days, over half our young people left school aged 16 without English and Maths at an acceptable standard. Some subjects were lucky if they hit 30% success at GCSE. At one stage, we were so busy locking down behaviour, that for some colleagues, a good lesson was one where the students sat still and didn't throw stuff.

Whether you are the head teacher, head of phase or head of department, the courage needed to sell your vision of the future when the present is a madhouse can sometimes escape you. I am not going to spend time here on how to lead a vision, you can google that, but I ask you to consider 'going big'!

What's the worst that could happen if you lead with a big vision in your sights? You may not get there. Ok.

What's the worst that could happen then if you lead with a tiny, obtainable, non-challenging vision in your sights? You get there. Your staff rest up and celebrate, and nobody has the inclination to push on for the next summit. This one feels nice, let's stay here for a bit!

Our situation had gone something like this:

-Behaviour was getting better, but was still a bit iffy.

-Teaching was getting better, but was still a bit iffy.

-Our reputation in the community was getting better, but was still a bit iffy.

Then, along comes Diana, spouting on about values and cornerstones, and then harping on about something to do with a vision of 'Every child a scholar'. I might as well have said, 'Every child will leave this school with 3 legs'. The confidence I had to even contemplate this vision was firmly rooted, because I knew that it could be achieved through the three steps of *I can work on my own, I can work through others, I can work with others.*

Truly, when I see that statement, I want to go back into headship all over again. I know, because I have done it myself, that nothing in leadership is impossible if you approach it through that concept.

Think of any situation you are dealing with in your leadership journey.
Visualise it.
Let the emotions attached to it rise within you.
Now answer these questions…

Is this something I should solve on my own?

Is this something I can solve through the skills of others?

Is this something I can solve working alongside others?

Every leadership issue can be solved using this method to start the leadership thinking.

I can work on my own

One thing that helped me deal with the loneliness of headship and the feelings of isolation that sometimes tried to overwhelm me, was this thought:

'Working on my own is a choice, it is not compulsory'.

When working alone, I would ask myself, *"Diana, are you working alone because that is what is expected, or because it is the best method for this task?"* Only if working on my was the best method, with a good reason as to why, would I then carry on. If, by asking this internal question the answer pointed out that I really should be working with, or through, others, I stopped and thought about another way forward. Try it, I promise it works.

Looking back, it's hard to think of situations where I did indeed work alone. Maybe it was all about the context, but the times were minimal.

However, I did spend time alone, starting the concept of leadership thinking; developing initial frameworks, setting the parameters, and reinforcing where things sat within the vision. Let me give you an example of a typical term-time Sunday afternoon in the Diana house.

Between 3 and 5pm on Sundays was my leadership thinking time (this method worked for me. I would try not to stress about things during the week, but just note them down for my Sunday afternoon thinking slot). I'd sit on the sofa in my conservatory, whack something inane on the TV to break up

the silence, and always be in reaching
distance of nibbles and drink at my side.
I'd sit and I'd think about stuff.

In one of those Sunday sessions, I
thought about the following:
What happens to my learning mentors
in school once they are qualified?
What is their career path?
How to they progress and aspire to the
next step?
What is the next step in mentoring?

I start with the leadership thinking. I do
this on my own and mull over the issue.
I am not thinking of solutions just yet,
but I am thinking of where the mentors

sit in the vision of school and the part they play to enhance it.

I imagine what school could be like if they were all 'master mentors', known for their expert practice and their next-level mentoring.

- What if the framework for their development included all being qualified to Degree level, and some to Masters level?
- What if their framework included training all staff in basic mentoring techniques?
- What if my mentors led a collaboration of mentors across the borough, so they have access

to support, advice and a network, just like the departmental teachers and leaders have?

- Who quality assures their work now? What is that information telling us?
- What do they see as the future of mentoring in our school?

I saw all of this as my responsibility to start or to deepen the leadership thinking concerning my school, and this I often did alone. However, it was by choice and not compulsory to work alone. I rapidly moved the thinking onto conversations with other leaders, and started working with or through my peers as soon as I could.

I can work through others.
We had a strong pastoral heart as a school and were skilful in caring for our young people, but our academic outcomes had to improve, and so when I became Head Teacher this was at the forefront of my vision. I wanted every child to be a scholar, to enjoy academia, and not to shy away because of perceptions, but to dive in and see what was there. I took the word 'scholar' in the loosest sense, meaning just to be good at studying and not giving up! It was the learners' choice what they

enjoyed, of course, but I wanted school to be a place where all the children could find something in the curriculum that they loved and could make their own.

Studying after school was something lots of our pupils struggled with. Lack of space or support at home, other responsibilities, the pull of a teenage social life, or lack of confidence. Something was usually in the way and our exam results suffered as a consequence. Two members of staff started tackling this issue directly, launching a strategic and well-thought out response, taking initiative and taking responsibility to make this part of the vision a reality. I was blown away.

At first, I had little knowledge of what they were doing, but they had found their place in the school vision, knew what was needed, and started work. *Aspirational, inspirational, mentoring,* or AIM, was born. It was so much more than just after-school revision. It was an efficient way of supporting young people with their studies and a tremendous investment by the whole school.

In the early days, Year 11 would try to leg it over the back fence rather than go to after-school classes, but they soon accepted what we were doing.

I could not afford to pay staff for their time on this project, but I don't think I even remember them ever asking. The idea of AIM days for staff reached me via some mutterings in the staff room. The proposal was that those who delivered AIM would get a dedicated morning or afternoon off timetable each week once Year 11 had left for the rest of the summer term. I thought "Grief, who is going to coordinate that?" As usual, working with others, a member of staff with a logical mind and an eye for detail stepped up to her place in the

vision and took charge. Taking on board
my parameters, she went away and made
it all happen.

Through support staff and pastoral
leaders.
Through teaching teams.
Through senior leaders.
Through the entire ethos, after-school
learning went through a revolution,
resulting in hundreds of pupils studying
after school and changing the narrative
of their lives one evening at a time. AIM
continued throughout my headship and
was a central pillar of our academic
success; all due to staff thriving in their
place within the vision.

When working through others,
everything is possible.

I can work with others.

I've told you that naturally I am an
introvert. I love shopping, holidaying,
and working on my own. However, at
work I am an advocate of great teams.
During my headship, there was so much
to do and so many needs to be met. The
reality of having young people's lives in
our hands weighed heavy on my
shoulders. I knew that we could not get
this wrong. Society is already a
minefield, and when you are young,
hailing from an underestimated
background and presenting as generally

unqualified, you are (how can I put this politely?), not exactly poised for success!

I am convinced that I had the senior team sent straight from Heaven. I loved them and poured myself into them, so they could go out and make the vision in my heart a live experience for our staff and students. The school was able to thrive because of the competence, commitment and love of the leaders around me. Being courageous as a leader... is choosing to work WITH others, allowing them to genuinely support alongside you, and carry with you the strategic and operational aspects of your vision. My team didn't work *for* me, they worked *with* me, and the difference between the two is subtle yet powerful.

As a position became available on the team for someone to lead on data (again), I went to national advert. Great candidates came for interview, and I was careful to devise tasks that would help me appoint both the skillset I was looking for and the kind of person that I could work with. One candidate was performing head and shoulders above his peers on the written and data tasks, and a clear lead had developed. Then he came into my office for the final task, the panel interview. He was so dreadful… I couldn't quite believe it! No confidence, shaking like a leaf, and when I asked the final question, he actually just put his head down and said in a quiet voice, *"I don't know anymore"*.

When he left, the governors just stared at me. I stared back. We had never seen anything like it! I threw my head back and laughed; one of those deep, belly-rolling laughs that makes others uncomfortable, but I didn't care. I had seen exactly what I needed in this nervous candidate, and now had to summon up the courage to tell the governors that he was the next best thing for the school. Yes really.

Courageous leaders are master relationship builders. You can work with anyone.

I knew that the lack of confidence and shaky presentation was all just interview faff. I had been watching the candidates all day; how they interacted with the students, how they treated my reception and catering staff, and what they said during social breaks. I pondered the questions they asked me to show their enthusiasm and ambition. I could tell a mile off those who had googled 'great questions to ask at interview' and those who were trying to get to know me. Based on it all, I knew that I could work with the shaky leaf candidate!

Shaky leaf was one of the most intelligent, articulate, strategic and hardworking leaders I have ever appointed in my career to date. He was a brilliant asset to the great team already in place, and his contribution was a strengthening pillar to my vision.

When you are carrying a vision to change the lives of young people through education, you have to be ready to achieve this with the hands of others. I didn't want people working for me, *I needed them to work with me.*

- Let the right answer come out of someone else's mouth

- Be gentle - you don't have to correct every mistake

- Let others show they are strong - step back so their light can shine

- If you see it, don't be afraid if it's not the finished article - make a start

- Tell them why and tell them again - that vision of the future has to be strong in everyone's mind

- Build teams so you can go big; what is the point in a small vision?

Interlude.

I am hoping you have noticed something important by this point. Please go back and read the 7 Courageous Statements again. The first two relating to fear and strength sound like they align directly with courage and leadership in challenging circumstances, and the rest sound…well, just normal? They don't have the same tone of 'courageousness' about them, and they don't seem as profound or Herculean. But they are. They all have their equal and valid place within the courageous leader. Together, they cemented my leadership journey and many areas of my life in general.

-When you have a great movie at your disposal as opposed to a good one, there are extra, almost unseen parts that determine the level of greatness.

-That musical score, which you didn't notice at the time, but is still running around in your head days later.

-The detail in the dialogue that captures you.

-The imagery that is still vivid when you leave the cinema.

All this extra stuff, tightly packed into 90 minutes of action, intrigue and plot that someone took countless days, weeks and months to get right.

From the outside, you get to enjoy the fruit of their labour; you consume, you benefit and you move on. They have put in months of 'grunt work'. Re-taking, editing, getting it right.

The courageous leader is not afraid to do the 'grunt work', as they recognise it is not all glory, but hours of doing the right thing at the right time that forms part of the fabric of their everyday leadership. It is the idea of 'grunt work and glory in leadership' that makes each of the 7 statements valid.

The courageous leaders are not superheroes strutting about with their pants on the outside of their trousers.

They are quietly resilient.

They are masters at building relationships.

They are advocates for those with small voices.

They are lovers of justice.

They are pursuers of the potential in others.

They are not afraid to cry, but steadfast in their resolve.

Just checking we are on the same page.

Procrastination will rob you of your destiny.

Love yourself more than that.

Diana Osagie

Chapter Four

I am human first and a
leader second.

I remember the
importance of family,
love, compassion and
grace.

July 2011

It's sports day. I am dressed in a tracksuit and trainers, lolloping about the place. I'm encouraging Year 7 as they race, cheering Year 8 as they jump in the sand, and dodging Year 10 as they fling the javelins around at will. It's the end of the toughest year in my leadership journey. Redundancies are over but I am still reeling from the toxicity that the situation gave birth to. I feel like I merely survived, and I hate that feeling. I want to _thrive_.

Just 'making it' tastes like failure to me.

I am internally still hurt at this point, but I have pushed that emotion down into a small box in my soul and hidden the key. Today, I am not a leader, I am merely a human!

Ridiculous, I know, but in those early days, I had not learnt to show up as my authentic self when the pressure was on.

I am a strong woman, so when pressure came, I tried to be super strong without vulnerability.

I am a competent woman, so when pressure came, I tried to be super competent with no flaws.

I am a knowledgeable woman, so when pressure came, I tried to be an encyclopaedia.

I am a courageous woman, so when pressure came, I tried to be super woman, unafraid of anyone or anything.

I am not surprised that I lost part of my humanity amidst all of this. I lost a part of myself that I loved and treasured. The part that made me laugh, made me feel warm, made me Diana.

Oh, I didn't tell you?

Ofsted had rocked up just before the sports day, and when I got the call, my heart stopped. I put the phone down to the Lead Inspector and fell to the floor in my office. As far as I was concerned, it was game over, and I would be sacked. I bawled my eyes out at the thought of what was to come. Fear rose up like one of those snakes that squeezes you to death. I couldn't see or hear anything except my own fear over an imagined scenario.

With this in mind… here's a nice acronym.

False

Evidence

Appearing

Real

This acronym will stay with me forever. When my mind goes into overdrive over 'what could be' rather than 'what actually is',

I have to remember that 'FEAR' may be at play, and say to myself, GET A GRIP!

I had no clue how to handle Ofsted, and no idea how a head teacher should lead a school through an inspection. I felt I was out of my depth in terms of knowledge, and had to call on reserves of resilience and sheer bloody mindedness in order to face it all.

My governors were great, my senior leaders were fabulous, and the middle leaders forgot they hated me as the Queen Cow of Redundancies, and rallied round for the sake of the school. The pupils were on point.

Ofsted was fine.

What did I do when I got home at the end of the inspection?

I collapsed, emotionally and physically exhausted onto my living room floor.

Sobbing.

Snot flowing.

Praying.

The relief, the release… I can't fully express it to you, even now. I lay on that carpet for ages, just trying to breathe and take in the fact that I had not died, that the school was still in one piece, and that things were ok.

Listen, if you take nothing else from this book, take this.

I chose the stupid route of attempting to take on a headship without proper coaching support. Yes, I had someone I went to see for an hour each half term, and he was great, but I couldn't call him and chat through how my personal talk was affecting my leadership walk! I didn't have an effective network outside of school, so I chose to interpret the concept of a head teacher as synonymous with 'lone figure who knows everything, can do everything, and sees ignorance as a weakness'.

Don't do what I did.

Leadership is an amazing privilege, and taking on a headship remains one of the best times and greatest honours of my life. I would do it again, but I'd also get support!

That sports day in July 2011 at the end of my first year as a head teacher at that school was the day I remember exhaling and returning slowly to my normal self.

I love the opportunities that I now have to teach leaders and to give key note speeches, and this part of the courageous statement gives rise to the most debate and conversation...*I understand the importance of family, grace, love and compassion.*

You have met those leaders who operate without love. They deliberately hurt others with their words, mistaking this for strength and leadership toughness.

You have served with those leaders who lead without compassion. They ensure you are docked half a day's pay because you had to go and arrange your mother's funeral one afternoon.

And as for grace (favour given to you… just because), you have worked with leaders who operate without it. They never give you anything, unless you fill out a form, give 100 reasons why, and justify the air you breathe.

Consider your own leadership. Where would you place yourself on the compassion, love and grace scale? More importantly, where would those who are subject to your leadership place you? It takes courage to have compassion, grace and love, in any form, at the heart of your leadership style.

It sounds weak?

It sounds ineffective?

It sounds like it belongs in a religious commune where you dance about wearing homemade linen, chanting mantras and eating only organic falafel?

It takes courage to love those who get on your nerves. It takes courage to be compassionate towards colleagues who just seem to take and take and only give the bare minimum back. I'm not saying allow anyone to walk over you, and I am definitely not saying to love people's foolishness, but I am saying that you have the choice to bark at someone in a meeting, or you can invite them into your office to hear the same message privately, before allowing them to leave with dignity.

We all love a good table…

Leading with grace, love and compassion

What is great	What will get on your nerves
You become really good at building relationships, as colleagues realise you are not just a witch that blew in on a broom, but are in fact human and have a heart	Some colleagues will take the bloody p**s and try to get one over on you all the time. (Go so far, then roar)

What is great	What will get on your nerves
You develop a culture of positive communication. Others begin to open up to you and share what makes them tick, where their commitment lies and the talents they have beyond their immediate role	It makes you somewhat vulnerable, as love and compassion means you open yourself up more to others.
You develop the courage to speak to your teams yourself. I refused to allow the union[2] to be my mouthpiece. I didn't allow another voice to represent or interpret mine. I shared my intentions, motives and ways of working openly.	Your armour is different in nature. You don't use negative email, be inflexible to the point of harm, show strict adherence to policy and procedure, or display an unapproachable manner to keep yourself at a safe distance.
	Instead you talk, listen and communicate. This is greater armour, and becomes more effective as you become more skilled in using it!

---

[2] I am not against unions, so don't bother to email me to rant! Everyone should belong to a union of some sort and they are important in the workplace, but they were not a bridge between my staff and me. My staff could come to me anytime with any issue and I went to them in the same way. Capability, disciplinary, sickness absence etc… I actively encouraged the union to play their role and offer support to my staff, but I didn't allow anybody to become my mouthpiece or create a 'them and us, leadership and workers' ethos in the organisation.

What is great	What will get on your nerves
The social, emotional and working capital you gain from colleagues is immense. They will go the extra mile and back with you, because of the way you lead them	Sometimes you feel as though you are not 'doing' anything worthwhile. This is because you are not *doing*, you are *being* - and that's ok.

I am so keen to make something clear here. Leading with love, compassion and grace is not a road to weak or ineffectual leadership. You can lead with authority, but still be known for your capacity to show love. Pace-setting leadership can be flavoured with compassion for others. Being democratic in your style still leaves room for you to extend grace to those who need it.

The first type of leader you are is a human one. Humans love, cry, hope, share, withstand adversity, celebrate with others and want the best for those around them. Be strong, be courageous, and most of all, be human. It's far easier than trying to be some sort of all-knowing, all-powerful leadership demi-god, believe me.

FAILURE IS A FEELING LONG
BEFORE IT'S A RESULT.

-MICHELLE OBAMA
BECOMING

Chapter Five

Leadership has weight.

I have the emotional
and physical strength
to carry it.

Ready for a wart?

I think I have trust issues.
Mic drop, exit stage left!

Seriously, I had to learn to trust again, as I had lost or supressed the natural trusting impulse humans have, and I know exactly when that natural trusting inclination left me.

2007, one of the worst years of my life. It tried to shape the woman and leader I would become. My husband decided that he would divorce me. Just for reference, we were married in front of 700 people, and my husband chose to divorce me by post.

My church imploded and then fell apart
(international ministry, scandal and
mess, so now I couldn't even pray
without crying).

My dad died.
What else can I say?

Every man I trusted with an important
part of my heart crumbled in their
position and left me stranded. I felt
abandoned, vulnerable and not sure how
to go about rebuilding the pieces of my
life. Yet, the mask I wore to work did
not slip once. I shared the pain with
myself, I got on by myself and I tried to
heal myself. Perhaps it would not have

been appropriate to share any of this with my team anyway, but trust me when I say, nobody had a clue that anything was amiss. I had no inclination about my own well-being, because we didn't really have that vocabulary back then. I looked after my staff because it was the moral thing to do, not because there was a book about it. Rarely did I think much about looking after myself. In September 2007, I was walking to the train station on my morning commute to school. I feel a piercing throb in the centre of my left calf. I wasn't in a position to check it and so promised myself I'd take a proper look once at school. The school day started, I got distracted, and I forgot about my leg. I went shopping that weekend for jeans, and found that NOTHING in the entire high street fitted me properly. I eventually spied a pair that looked promising in the Marks and Spencer 'classic' range (I think legally you have to be retired to wear these, but needs must). I turned and caught sight of my calf in the mirror and gasped at the bulging mass that was throbbing beneath my skin.

I was 36 years old.

I was newly divorced.

I was fatter than I had ever been, trying to shove my belly into size 22 jeans.

As a testament to the amount that I had let myself go physically, I was now the owner of a very sinister looking varicose vein. Those things are never great.

I needed help, but I didn't know it. I was in need of support, advice and friendship, but I kept myself in a solitary place because of emotional pain. I was carrying increasingly greater leadership weight, but I had no appreciation of the level of physical and emotional health that was needed to carry it successfully. My personal circumstance led to a tear in my emotional resilience, and so by the time I was appointed to the position of a head teacher, this meant I took words from others very personally. I digested every criticism, success, failure and piece of negativity levelled at the school as though they were personal critiques. Words of the naysayers within the community weighed heavily on my shoulders, and so emotionally, I took on weight that was not even mine.

Leadership is a privilege in our schools, where the future of young peoples' lives is in our hands. School leaders carry a burden for society that is rarely celebrated by our political leaders, and remains the subject of banter with others who still hilariously say in jest,

"Yeah, but you get all those holidays, don't you…"

For those of you like me who choose to serve in challenging contexts, advocating for excellence in circumstances that scream hopelessness, the fifth courageous statement is especially for you, so let me break it into 3 parts.

Leadership has weight. Don't attempt to carry it alone. Distribute the weight into the capable hands of those around you. If you cannot see them, you are either not looking hard enough, or are looking with a blinding bias in your sight. Don't be a hero and do it all yourself. Nobody will thank you for it, and your colleagues will resent the fact that you don't allow others to develop their leadership muscle. They'll think you only delegate things that don't matter.

When it's time to let something go, let it go. Don't stagger under unnecessary weight because that's the way it has always been done. If the horse is dead, don't carry it on your back! Dismount, get a new horse, or walk. When it's time to put the weight down and switch off, do so, and don't entertain the ridiculous guilt that seems to come when you turn your phone off or don't respond within milliseconds to every email.

Leadership demands emotional strength. One of the most emotionally strong leaders I ever met was Miss Zackerwich, my head teacher when I was in secondary school as a pupil. 4ft 9in tall and about 3ft wide, she was a powerhouse that kept a 1500-pupil girls' school in south London in check. Prolonged nationwide strike action, dilapidated facilities, staff of over 300 (number, not age), this woman showed an emotional health and strength that has left a lasting impression on me. I remember when she told us in assembly that it's ok to cry (one of the girls in school had passed away suddenly). In fact, she told us we could all cry right there if we wanted to. So, we did, all 1500 of us. She cried, too.

Your colleagues will pursue emotional health, so as you build others, build yourself, too. Network like a professional. Go beyond your academy or trust, seek professional support and hear the voices of others who have a clean and objective motive towards you. I have said it before, engage with quality coaching for yourself. If you need to go one step further and access counselling then do so. Don't hesitate, don't be embarrassed. You are not obliged to shout it from the roof, but you are obliged to look after yourself.

If you don't know something, and you really need or want to know it, then ask for help. The hours I wasted trying to work out school finance spreadsheets and budgets, incomings and outgoings, or whatever they were… Finally, I rang the Local Authority and said, "Martin, I need help, I haven't the foggiest what's going on, my business manager has tried to explain it, and I still don't get it. Please come to school, sit with me, and show me slowly how this works". Martin ended up coming to see me three times. I couldn't be bothered to be afraid of how it might look to him or anyone else. I just needed help, and by asking for it, I got it. Job done.

Leadership demands physical strength. Simply put, leadership is knackering. It will take a toll on your body and you need to mitigate against this via health and fitness if you don't want to pay for the damage in the long term. I wish I could say that after the varicose vein fiasco, I got rid of my size 22 belly and turned into a fitter, leaner version of my fabulous self.

Nope, I did not.

What followed was a decade of ill–health and nonsense. One thing after another. But, I will never, as I write this, give up the pursuit of a healthier lifestyle and bikini body… The kebabs are not helping though!

I'm not going to tell you how to get fit or stay healthy, you can google that. Can you tell I love to google? I will, however, tell you that procrastination with this agenda in your life is a mug's game.

Love yourself enough, take care of yourself.

In the future, there will be no female leaders. There will just be leaders.

Sheryl Sandberg

Chapter Six

I am accurate and exacting.

If it's going to be done, then let's do it right.

This is a short chapter. The message here is easy to say but can be hard to do. It's part of the leadership grunt work I mentioned some pages back. If your colleagues would say that any of the following can be said about you, then you (perhaps unknowingly) are the source of stress for those under your leadership.

- 'You never know where you are with him/her'
- 'The goal posts are always changing. One minute they want it like this, the next minute they want it like that'

- 'You never know how he/she will react… you have to be so careful around him/her'
- 'Their reaction depends on who you are'

If staff spend part of their time trying to gauge who you are as their leader and how they should react when you are around, then courageous statement six will be a tough one for you! *I am accurate and exacting. If it's going to be done, then let's do it right.* For this to be true, you need to consistently communicate a message of quality and clarity, enabling all stakeholders to find their place within the vision, understand the nature and level of their contribution to the daily life of the school, and have the tools, policies and procedures that enable them to contribute with quality and not mediocrity. Sometimes, leaders make it hard for others to be good!

What do you want?

Why do you want it?

What is the purpose of it?

How do you want it done?

What might success look like?

Remember my Sunday leadership thinking time? Often these 5 questions framed those 2 hours.

Then, I would take my answers back to SLT for them to play around with and shape, before then heading to the MLT.

Did you notice I said, *"I take my answers back to SLT...?"* I don't send them an email or issue a bulletin on Monday morning. Even a well-crafted email will still leave room for interpretation, questions and queries.

I never experienced a whole department all producing quality outcomes the way I expected because I sent them an email or issued a new policy.

If you want accuracy, quality and consistency, the investment in the relationship has to be high. Talking, listening, re- framing and re- working comes first - *then* confirm it all in an email!

Can I share a tip with you?

You have to be able to say no and to be comfortable in the silence that follows. Don't fill the space with apology or platitudes. Sometimes, things are simply not good enough, and someone needs to say "No".

- Reports going to parents intended to give a picture of their child's progress, but instead are filled with meaningless statements chosen on a whim from a bank.
- Year 11 after-school revision programmes that pull the student from pillar to post, putting them in impossible situations as they

have to choose which teacher to satisfy and attend their session.

- Some staff subject to sickness policy the moment they hit 8 days, whilst others rack up 20 days and nobody says anything.

Leaders; if we are going to do this, then let's do it right. Let's be honest and fair in our approach. When it's not right, say so, but as much as you can, allow your community to be part of the answer. Be known for wanting quality, but being reasonable in how that quality is obtained.

Interlude

Can we talk about love?

Early on, I didn't have a philosophy for building or developing my senior team, I just chose to love them.

I thrive when I am loved. I relax and fulfil the potential of every day when I feel loved. I am better equipped to handle pressure and challenging circumstances knowing those around me love me.

I realised early on, that to be successful at leading my school community in a challenging urban context, I needed to have a senior team that had no problem being fabulous and operating at the top of their game. Through them, the middle leaders could be supported to develop in strength and operate at the top of *their* game. Through this strong middle, the teaching, support and administration staff could also reach their potential. For me, it always comes back to the quality of the senior leadership team, because if the leadership at this level is poor or the capacity to improve is low, then any school will struggle to keep its head above water, let alone swim in the strong currents of urban education.

Let's assume that love is defined as 'affectual concern for the well- being of others', choosing to love my team through all circumstances remains the best leadership decision I have ever made.

Love looked like this…

Physical love: This cost me personally about £1k per year.

-Birthday cards and gifts for every senior leader, every year.

-Dinner on me for the whole team, three times a year.

-Personal Christmas gifts every year.

-Sweeties, chocolates, random cute things appearing on their desks…

-Weekly SLT meetings with fruit platters & specialised coffee.

Emotional love: No cost to me, just a time commitment.

-Every day, of every week, we would have lunch together after dining hall duty. It was our time to laugh, chill and relax with each other for 20 minutes. It was a highlight of the day not to be missed.

-Outside of line management meetings, a scheduled one-hour meeting with every member of SLT each half term. We would sit and talk in private, one to one.

-Anytime, any day, at home, at school… my team could call me. They rarely did, but when that call came late in the evening, I would always take it and respond to help.

-They needed time to deal with a family issue? My response was always 'GO'.

-Their little one was appearing in the Nativity? My response was to tell them to go and be present.

-They needed support? Whatever I could do, I would.

"Tell me what you need so you can be awesome, and I will do my best to give it to you."

Lots of this I was able to extend to my middle leadership team and to the staff at large, but it started with the idea of professional love for the senior team close to me, and filtered through from there.

Because of love, I learned to seek out my SLT, ask their advice and lean on them for support. I learned to push them forward when success came, and I stepped forward when the s**t hit the fan! I couldn't do anything outside of my team, but with them, so much was possible. I owe my success as a head teacher to my senior team.

I left school a few years ago… but I love them still.

"THE QUESTION
ISN'T WHO'S
GOING TO LET ME;
IT'S WHO'S GOING
TO STOP ME."

-Ayn Rand

Chapter Seven

I am relentlessly consistent on things that matter.

I have developed insight into what matters.

It's the final chapter, so let me bring it home. This is where the grunt work leads to those glory moments that make leadership such a fulfilling vocation. Let me illustrate a grunt and glory circumstance.

My governors (who were fantastically brilliant and useful) worked tirelessly to get the new school buildings planned and built with our contractors. The deputy head, the previous head, me as the new head, and at some stage every single member of the leadership team, were involved in trying to get the whole thing built! Ah, but hold on…

We are not a bog standard comprehensive; we are an Arts and Media specialist school, where every child is entitled to study a creative arts curriculum alongside their traditional subjects for their entire school career. We were committed to this ethos of having creativity at the heart of the curriculum; not just championing the odd dance troupe rocking up to entertain the kids, but a full-on educational arts experience for every child - every day.

We were a school in the heart of London surrounded by wealth and poverty. 2/3 of my families could not afford to pay for a school lunch, so many of my pupils were labelled as disadvantaged[3]. However, they attended this local school which had great science labs, sprung floors in the dance studios, an Astroturf pitch for sport, and art spaces Picasso would have envied. All of this – creating buildings, planning facilities, designing a curriculum, and sourcing great staff for every subject - was the grunt grunt grunt of leadership. The glory? Here's a glimpse.

It was lunchtime, and normally, I'd have been on duty in the hall, but on this particular day, I was wandering about on

---

[3] I hated this term, but that is what they were called. Disadvantaged pupils nationwide performed less well than their peers, and schools across the country struggled to close the gap in attainment for these pupils. We managed to do it, but it was not easy.

the 2nd floor, when I heard music coming from one of the dance studios. I peered through the glass window of the door, and at the end of the studio I saw two Year 8 girls, (let's call them Maryam and Josie).

Josie was from a large traveller family who lived on the local estate. Lovely girl, bit gobby, but bright and always ready to take on a challenge (she once decked a Year 10 lad who said something about her mum). Maryam barely ever spoke. She was Somali and had not yet learnt enough English to make herself understood. She lived on the same estate as Josie, but stayed late every day at school to get to grips with the English curriculum.

Josie and Maryam sat on the floor of the dance studio, shoes and socks off. Maryam had put her head scarf in the corner and both girls twiddled and twaddled about to music from the little stereo they had borrowed from somewhere. Some sort of dance routine that included Beyoncé moves and a bit of ballet thrown in for good measure. It mesmerised me.

These two girls, living in North London, going to their local secondary school, completely unaware of the leadership grunt that underpins their ability to pursue their dreams to dance... This, my friends, was a glimpse of glory.

Be relentlessly consistent on the things that matter. In this instance, it was the curriculum that mattered. It always does. The educational experience we offer in every subject, the after-school clubs and extra-curricular trips we run... it all matters. 15 years before Ofsted[4] released a framework to judge schools, which included a focus relating to the curriculum, schools up and down the country had decided for themselves that this mattered and had designed and

---

[4] The system of regulation and judgement of school standards is the responsibility of Ofsted. In 2019, a new framework to inspect schools was released that gave focus to curriculum intent, implementation and impact. Many educationalists including myself welcomed the new stance.

implemented curriculums that changed young peoples' lives and gave them access to an alternative narrative different to their home circumstance.

What matters to you?

Think about it.

Articulate it.

Stand for it.

Courageous leaders develop insight into what matters and have the tenacity to push and defend what is important. Creative subjects in secondary education came under threat by government action when they decided that schools would be judged in league tables by a qualification[5] that **excluded** all creative and technological subjects. Overnight, the heart of our curriculum seemed to hold no value to the outside world, and I found myself as the head teacher having to defend our stance to outside voices. I sat in head teachers' meetings where I could hear the 'joke', *"What's the point in your school now? The arts are dead at GCSE and E-Bacc. Proper subjects reign!"*

My governors, my SLT, me... were all adamant that our curriculum as it stood was valuable and that we would make

---

[5] The English Baccalaureate instituted by Michael Gove (secretary of state for education 2010- 14) measured all secondary schools by their performance at GCSE in English, Maths, Science, Humanities and Modern Languages. The consequences of omitting the arts and technology still plays out in our schools today.

things happen – E-Bacc or not. Every subject had its place in our school at GCSE and it took courage to stand by this belief.

Friends; please decide what matters in your leadership. Seek consensus with your teams on the things that matter.

If it's important; then be courageous and don't let it go.

The end?

It had better not be!

I want you to be encouraged, strengthened, and to have clarity on a path to leading with courage. I'm sharing with you what I have learnt so far, but my own journey continues.

I hope you recognised yourself in some of the courageous statements? Remember, it's not about heroism. It's that resilient human leader who loves their team and who advocates for the greatness in others.

Let's stay connected.

Diana   x

Stay connected...
www.courageousleadership.co.uk

- Subscribe to weekly coaching
  videos you can stream
  24/7 that support you with
  workable strategies for leadership
  challenges (how the heck do I
  have that difficult conversation...
  I have a nutter on my team who

keeps undermining me, my staff have walked out on strike, I think I am rubbish at my job and someone is bound to notice, that sort of stuff).

- Access webinar courses for you and /or your team (building effective teams, overcoming resistance in the workplace, developing yourself as a leader etc.)
- Request face to face or online coaching
- Request leadership team training
- Say, 'Diana! Please come and do a key note speech at my event!'

About the author…

DIANA OSAGIE

With 16 years of experience leading
secondary education, including six years
as a successful head teacher in a London
secondary school, Diana works at the
cutting edge of leadership development
and school improvement. She is known

as a resilient school leader, and is skilled in urban leadership under challenging circumstances.

Diana has enjoyed substantial success in developing school-wide models that strategically enhance the quality of teaching and learning across the curriculum, and can couple sound strategic vision whilst giving clear operational direction. She lectures on a MA in Educational Leadership for a UK university, and is also a school assessor with developed expertise of scrutinising school-wide systems.

With a proven track record of developing leaders via bespoke training programmes, Diana specialises in supporting organisations to grow their leadership culture in order for existing and emerging leaders to improve and flourish. She has established capability in mentoring and in supporting leaders facing challenging circumstances and change.

Successful leaders have someone in their corner who understands and has overcome similar challenges. We all need an advocate…and that's what Diana becomes when you work together...*an advocate for your leadership.*

(She likes UFC, Haribo sweets and kebabs...in any order)

Made in the USA
Middletown, DE
23 March 2021